BUILDING BLOCKS OF COMPUTER SCIENCE

ORGANIZING DATA

Written by Echo Elise González

Illustrated by Graham Ross

a Scott Fetzer company
Chicago

World Book, Inc.
180 North LaSalle Street
Suite 900
Chicago, Illinois 60601
USA

For information about other World Book publications, visit our website at **www.worldbook.com** or call **1-800-WORLDBK (967-5325)**.
For information about sales to schools and libraries, call 1-800-975-3250 (United States), or 1-800-837-5365 (Canada).

Library of Congress Cataloging-in-Publication Data for this volume has been applied for.

Building Blocks of Computer Science
ISBN: 978-0-7166-2883-5 (set, hc.)

Organizing Data
ISBN: 978-0-7166-2889-7 (hc.)

Also available as:
ISBN: 978-0-7166-2897-2 (e-book)

1st printing August 2020

Acknowledgments:
Art by Graham Ross/The Bright Agency
Series reviewed by Peter Jang/Actualize Coding Bootcamp

TABLE OF CONTENTS

There is a glossary on page 30. Terms defined in the glossary are in type **that looks like this** on their first appearance.

DATA IS INFORMATION
Computer programs use a lot of **data.**
Data is information that a computer can store and use.
The way information is stored is important.
Making a computer program means storing a lot of information.

I'm a kind of **data structure.**

DATA STRUCTURE

WHAT IS A DATA STRUCTURE?
A **data value** is a small, simple piece of information.
Little pieces of information are easy to store in a program's code. Like an apple being stored in a basket, a value can be stored in a **variable**.
But, storing large amounts of information can be trickier.
That's where **data structures** come in handy!

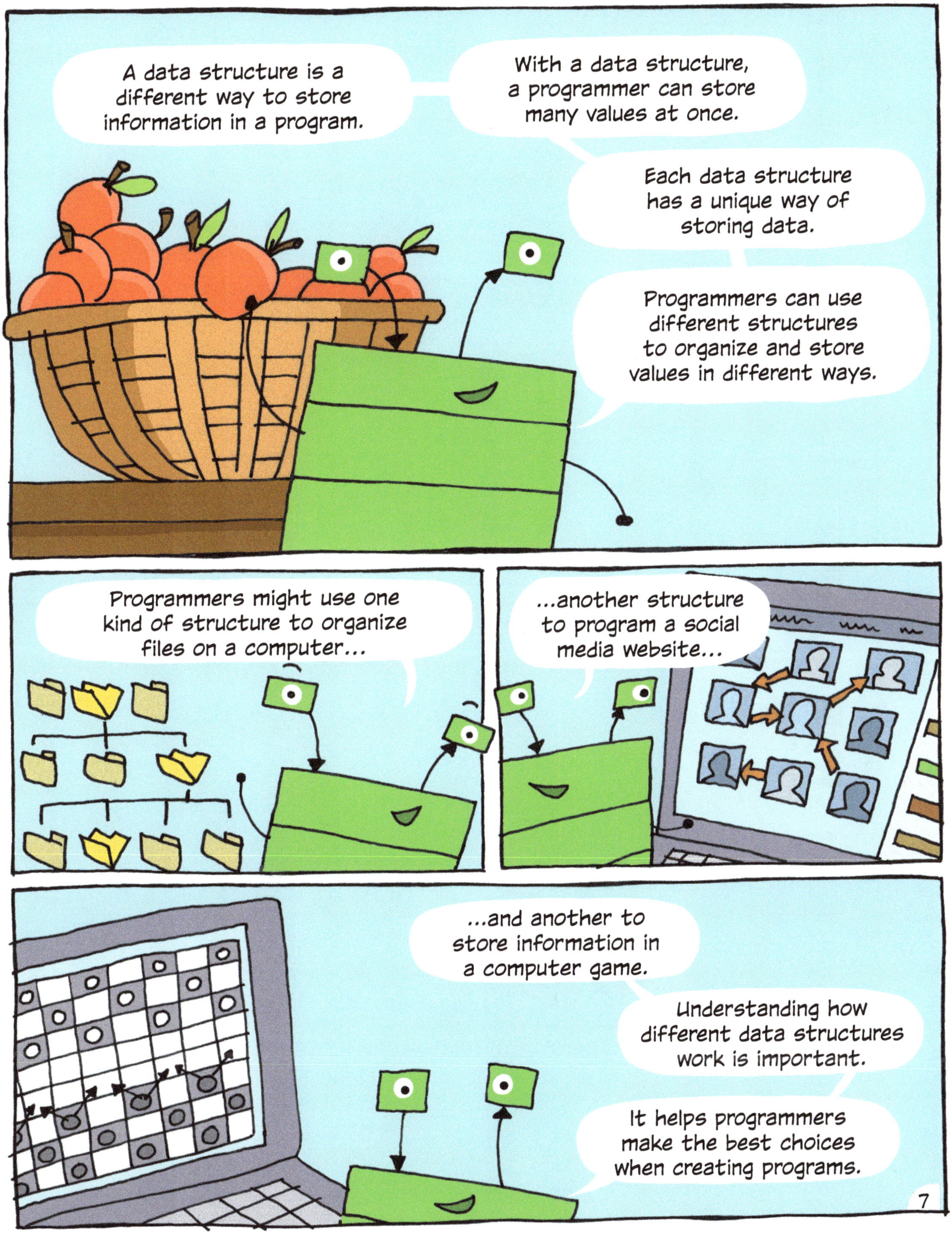

A data structure is a different way to store information in a program.

With a data structure, a programmer can store many values at once.

Each data structure has a unique way of storing data.

Programmers can use different structures to organize and store values in different ways.

Programmers might use one kind of structure to organize files on a computer...

...another structure to program a social media website...

Let's say I want to store information about this unicorn.
body = "pink"
I can make one **variable** to store its body color...
horn = "white"
One to store the color of its horn...

wings="blue"
And one to store the color of its wings.
I can use a **structure** to put all of these variables into one variable.
I'm going to call this structure variable "unicorn1."
unicorn1={body:"pink",horn:"white",wings:"blue"}
Now, all the information I have stored about this unicorn fits in the "unicorn1" structure!

unicorn1,={body:"pink",
horn:"white, wings:"blue"}

This other unicorn has no wings, so I can't use the same **structure** that I used for the first unicorn.

I'll make a new structure!

unicorn2={body:"green", horn:"yellow", gem:"purple"}

I'll replace the "wings" **variable** with a "gem" variable in my new structure.

unicorn1={body:"pink", horn:"white", wings:"blue"}

unicorn2={body:"green", horn:"yellow", gem:"purple"}

I can use structures with different sets of variables to store different kinds of information about the unicorns.

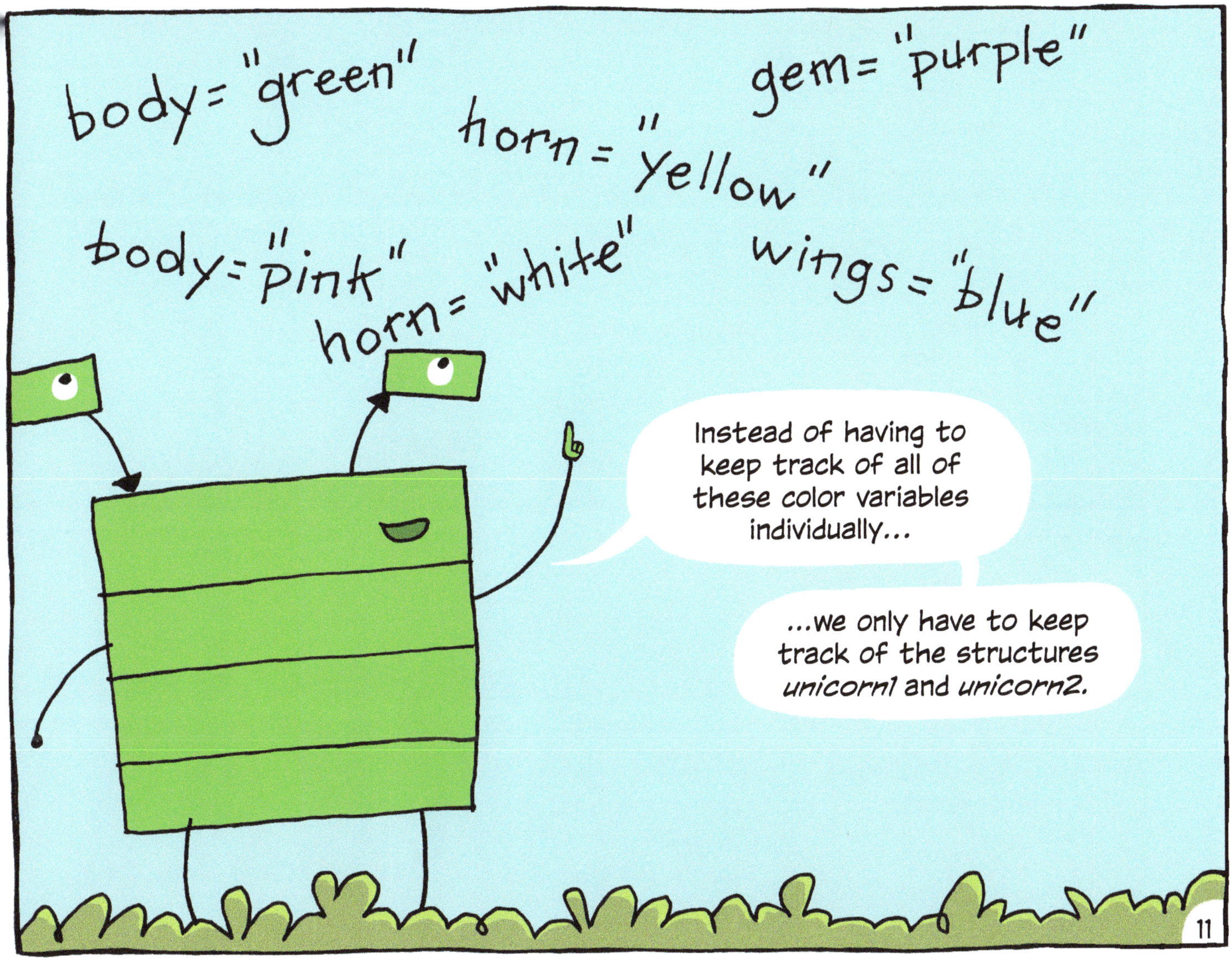

body="green"

horn="yellow"

gem="purple"

body="pink"

horn="white"

wings="blue"

Instead of having to keep track of all of these color variables individually...

...we only have to keep track of the structures *unicorn1* and *unicorn2*.

ARRAYS

unicorn2={body:"green", horn:"yellow",
gem:"purple"}

unicorn5={body:"blue", horn:"orange",
wings:"green"}

Unicorns galore!

I can also use a **data structure** to put all of the unicorns into one bigger structure.

I'll use an **array** data structure to store them all.

An array stores a sequence of related information.

I'm going to name my array "all_unicorns."

all_unicorns

All_unicorns=[unicorn1, unicorn2, unicorn3, unicorn4, unicorn5]

There are 5 unicorns, so I'll use 5 **elements** in the array.

An element is one piece of the array. It can store one piece of information.

Each element stores all the information about one of the unicorns.

It's all neatly stored in the array!

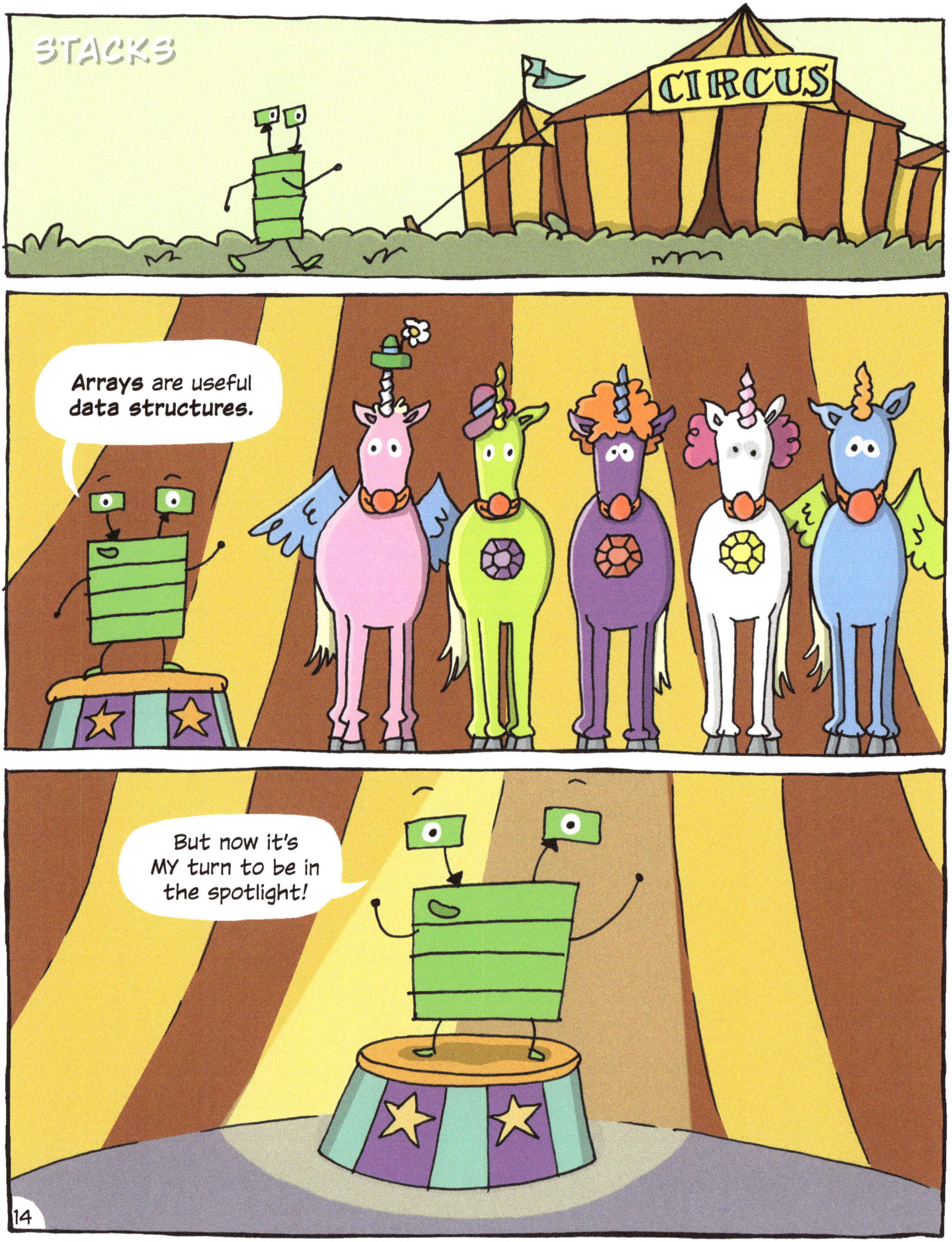

STACKS

Arrays are useful **data structures.**

But now it's MY turn to be in the spotlight!

So, what exactly is a **stack**?
STACK
Well... I'm a data structure that's similar to a stack or pile of things.
SPROING
WOBBLE
Data can only be added to the top of a stack.
It can only be removed from the top of the stack, too.
For this reason, programmers sometimes describe stacks as "Last In, First Out."
The last **element** that was added to a stack is also the first element to be removed.
THUD

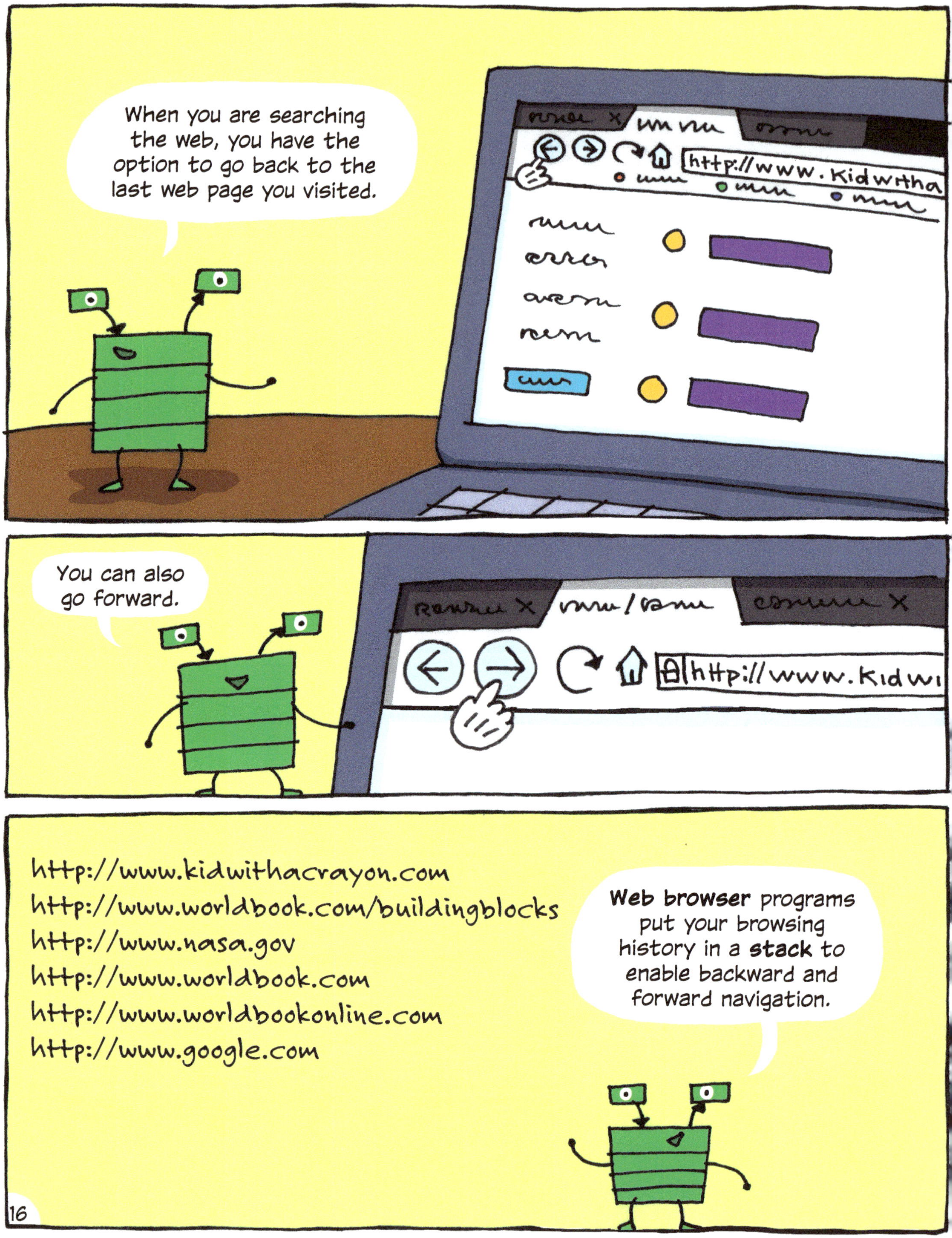

When you are searching the web, you have the option to go back to the last web page you visited.

http://www.kidwithacrayon.com
http://www.worldbook.com/buildingblocks
http://www.nasa.gov
http://www.worldbook.com
http://www.worldbookonline.com
http://www.google.com

Web browser programs put your browsing history in a **stack** to enable backward and forward navigation.

When you are browsing the internet, the **URL's** from the web pages you visit are stored in this stack.

http://www.kidwithacrayon.com
http://www.worldbook.com/buildingblocks
http://www.nasa.gov
http://www.worldbook.com
http://www.worldbookonline.com
http://www.google.com

So, when you want to go back, you can visit the URL's one at a time, starting at the top of the stack.

http://www.kidwithacrayon.com
http://www.worldbook.com/buildingblocks
http://www.nasa.gov
http://www.worldbook.com
http://www.worldbookonline.com
http://www.google.com

Other programs use stacks in similar ways.

http://www.worldbook.com/buildingblocks

For example, hitting the "undo" button in a **word processing program** causes the program to go back through the stack of actions it has stored.

Enchanted Ice Cream
A **queue** is also good for storing **data** in an orderly, predictable way.

QUEUE
Queue is pronounced *kyoo*, like the letter Q.

Programmers sometimes describe a queue as "First In, First Out."

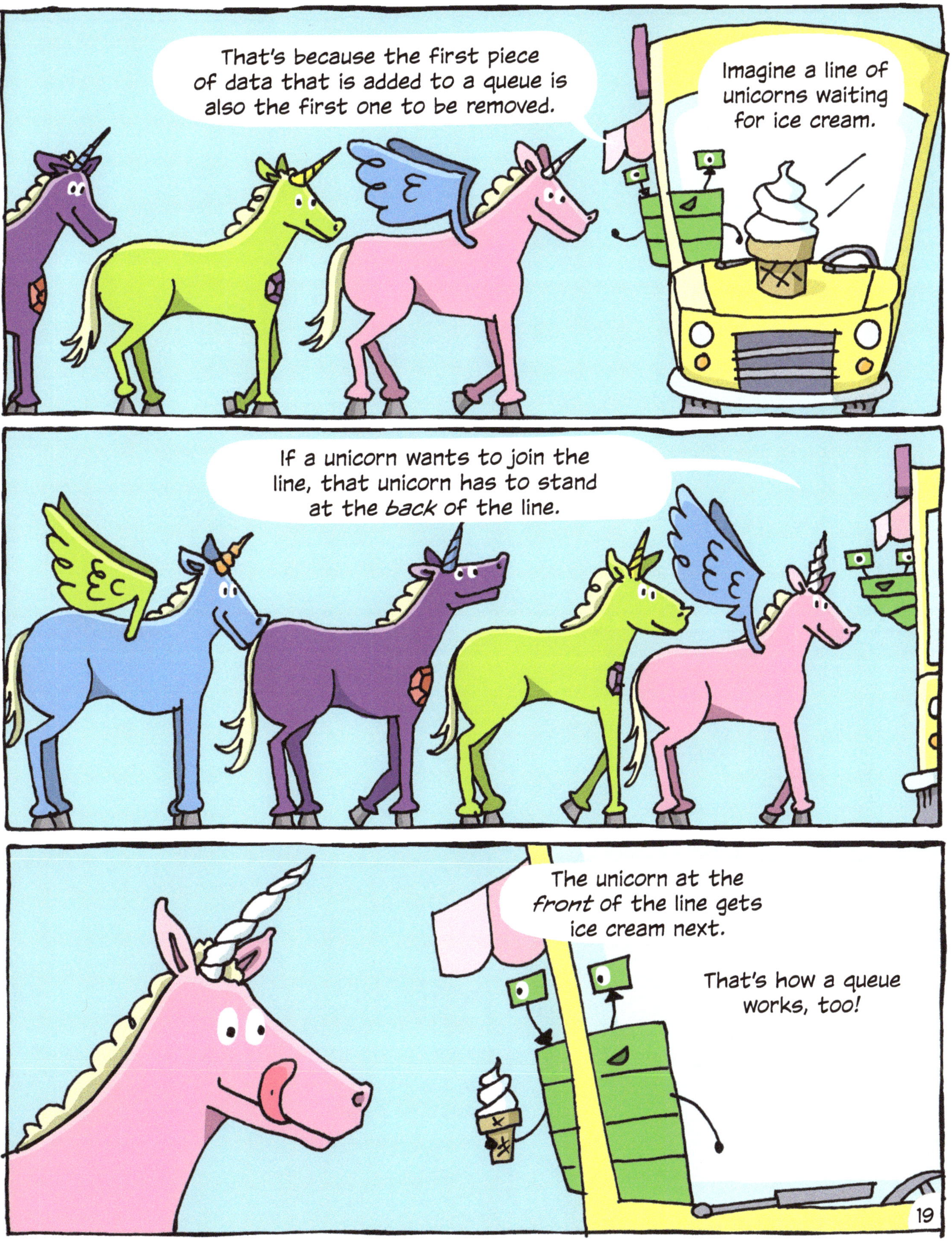

That's because the first piece of data that is added to a queue is also the first one to be removed.

Imagine a line of unicorns waiting for ice cream.

If a unicorn wants to join the line, that unicorn has to stand at the *back* of the line.

I made a comic book on the computer!
POW!
PING
PRINT
Now, I want to print out the pages.
TAP

It's important for the pages to print out in the correct order, so the story doesn't get jumbled.
1
2
3
1 2
3 4
5 6
7 8
The computer and the printer use a **queue data structure** to keep the pages in the right order.
Just like the unicorns waiting in line for ice cream, each page has to wait to be printed in the proper order.

Enchant
I want to keep track of all the ice cream flavors that we have here at Enchanted Ice Cream.
I can use a **set data structure** to do that.
In a set, all the pieces of information are stored in just one **variable.**
ice_cream_flavors=Set(["chocolate", "vanilla", "strawberry"])
I named my variable "ice_cream_flavors." It tells me all the different flavors that we have.
We have chocolate, vanilla, and strawberry.
I'm making a new flavor today: mint!

ice_cream_flavors=Set(["chocolate", "vanilla", "strawberry", "mint"])
All I have to do is add "mint" to my ice_cream_flavors set. Easy!
It doesn't matter how many mint scoops we have... They all fit into one element—the mint element!

Have you ever made a playlist of songs or videos on the computer or on your phone?

If you have, you were probably using a **set data structure** without knowing it!

Many programs use this structure to organize sets of information.

my_favorite_songs = Set(["Yankee Doodle", "The Stacks of My Tears"])

YANKEE DOODLE

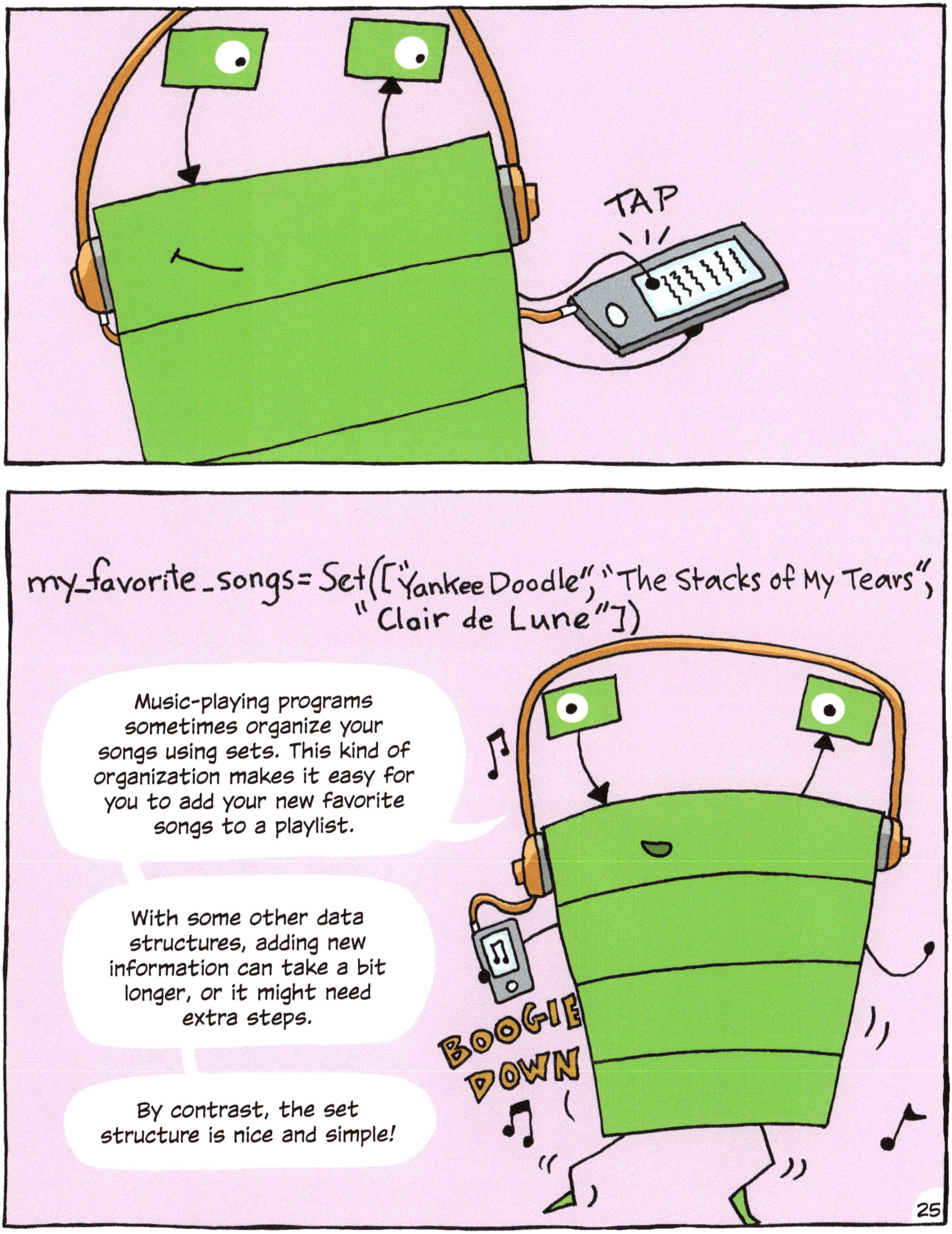

TAP

my_favorite_songs = Set(["Yankee Doodle", "The Stacks of My Tears", "Clair de Lune"])

Music-playing programs sometimes organize your songs using sets. This kind of organization makes it easy for you to add your new favorite songs to a playlist.

With some other data structures, adding new information can take a bit longer, or it might need extra steps.

By contrast, the set structure is nice and simple!

I can use a **hash structure** to do this.

HASH

A hash links each **element** to a matching piece of information. A hash structure shows how the **data** is related.
Hashes can be useful when we have two groups of information that need to be linked together.

When you're making a computer program, it is important to think about the best way to organize information.
Some computer programs need a **structure** that keeps **data** in an orderly line.
Some need a structure that shows how data is related.

And some programs just need a simple structure that holds all the necessary information.

DRIVE·THRU

ice cream

Knowing all about data structures is a big step to becoming a great programmer!

GLOSSARY

array a data structure that stores a collection of related information.

data information that a computer processes or stores.

data structure the organization of data by a computer program.

data value a number or other piece of information that is used in a computer program.

element the smallest part of a data structure. It can store one piece of information.

hash a data structure that links each element to a matching piece of data.

queue (kyoo) a data structure in which data is removed from a list in the same order that it was added.

set a data structure that stores all of the data in one variable.

stack a data structure in which data can only be removed from a list in the reverse order that it was added.

structure (see data structure)

URL (Uniform Resource Locator) the address of a website. A URL is also called a web address.

variable a value, or piece of information, that can change.

web browser a program that finds and displays web pages and other information from the internet.

word processing program a program that enables the user to compose and edit written documents.

GO ONLINE

Can you use a data structure to find the unicorns' missing pets? Go to this website to try it out! Click on the Match the Missing Pet activity. You'll also find lots of other fun computer science activities!

www.worldbook.com/BuildingBlocks

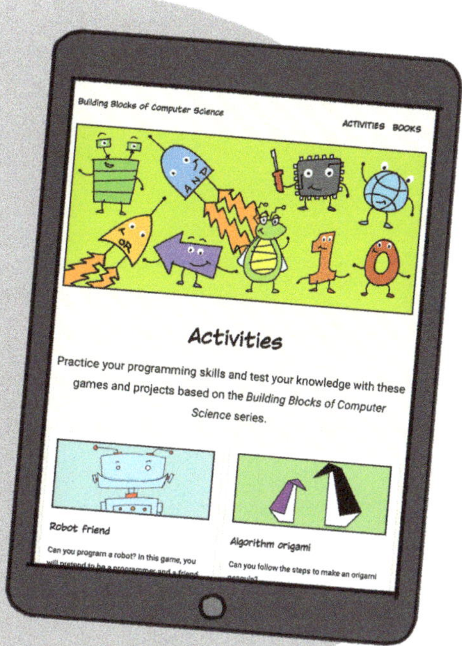

INDEX

www.ingramcontent.com/pod-product-compliance
Ingram Content Group UK Ltd.
Pitfield, Milton Keynes, MK11 3LW, UK
UKHW061958290726
14090UKWH00021B/1269